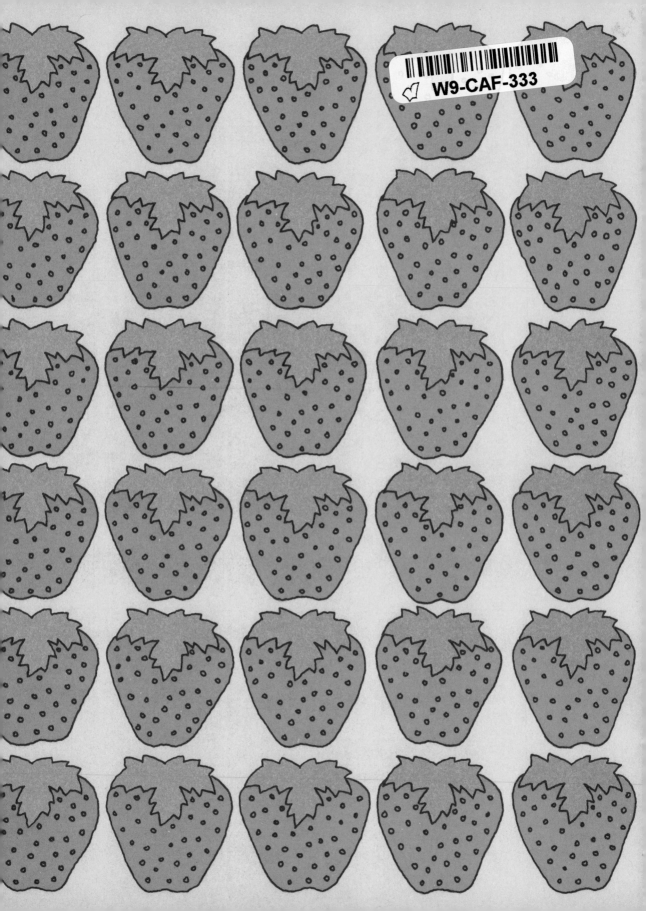

THE STICKYBEAR FAMILY ™

Bedford Stickybear   **Sara Stickybear**

Bumper Stickybear

Kristen

this
**strawberry library
of first learning
book
belongs to**

Megan

Cook

Stickybear™ is the registered trademark of Optimum Resource, Inc.
Strawberry® and A Strawberry Book® are the registered
trademarks of One Strawberry, Inc.

Weekly Reader Books' Edition

Library of Congress Cataloging in Publication Data

Hefter, Richard.
Watch out!

(Stickybear books)
"Weekly Reader Books' edition."
Summary: Stickybear teaches Bumper the meaning of
various signs and how they help keep everyone safe.
1. Safety education – Juvenile literature.
[1. Safety.   2. Signs and symbols]   I. Title.
II. Series: Hefter, Richard.   Stickybear books.
HV675.5.H43   1983   363.1   83-2190
ISBN 0-911787-03-8

the stickybear™ book of safety

watch out!

by Richard Hefter

Optimum Resource, Inc. • Connecticut

Stickybear is teaching Bumper about signs and safety.

This sign tells cars and bikes to stop here.

A red light means stop.

A yellow light is a warning.   A green light means go.

This sign means stay out.

This sign means stay out too.

This sign warns us to watch out for trains.

Watch out!
Be careful!
Here is another warning.

We go in here!

We come out here!

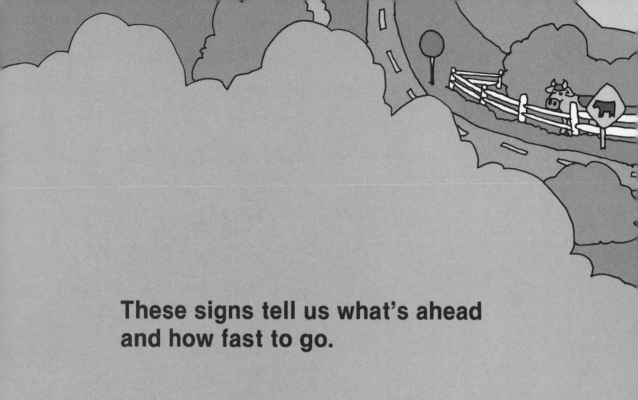

These signs tell us what's ahead
and how fast to go.

Always obey this sign even on a hot day.

Watch out!
There must be thin ice here.
We had better keep off.

Do you know what this sign means?

Yes, it means NO FUN!

NO
RUNNING
JUMPING
PICNICS
BALL PLAYING
BICYCLES
LITTERING
LOITERING
RADIOS

You should always read the signs!

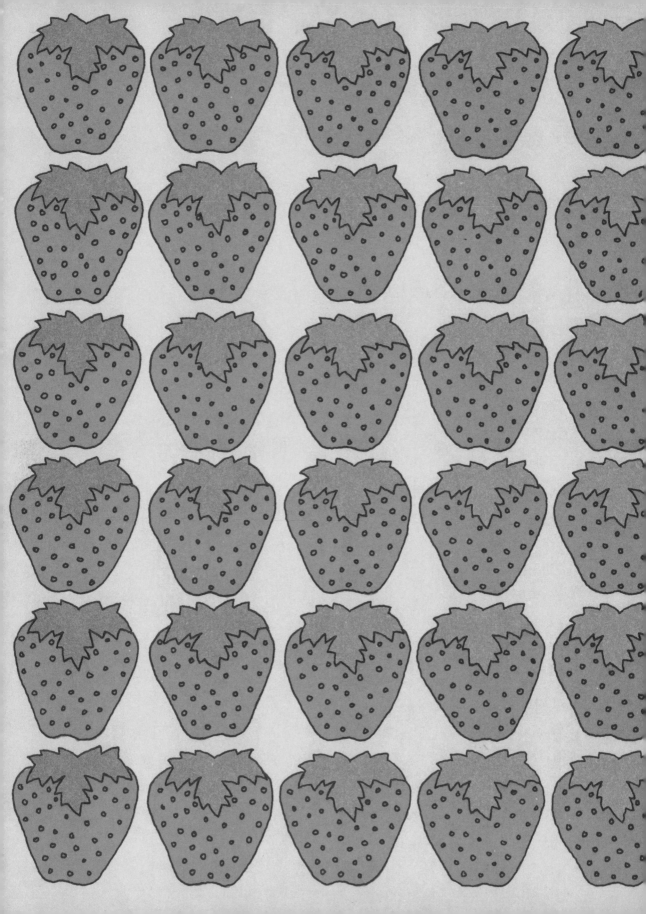